BLINK!

verb
1: to shut and open the eyes quickly
2: to shine intermittently or unsteadily (or: with a
   light that goes on and off)
noun
1: an act of shutting and opening the eyes quickly
2: a momentary gleam of light

Doe Boyle

illustrated by
Adèle Leyris

Albert Whitman & Company
Chicago, Illinois

Eyesight is the ability to see.
Sight relies on light—and the eye.
Our eyes make images
that help us make sense of our world.
Each eye is the sum of its parts.
No part works well without the help of the others:
the lens, the iris, the pupil, the sclera,
the choroid, the cornea, the vitreous humor,
the retina, too, with its rods and its cones—
and several parts more—in most living creatures.
Blink.
Blink-blink.
Or no blink.

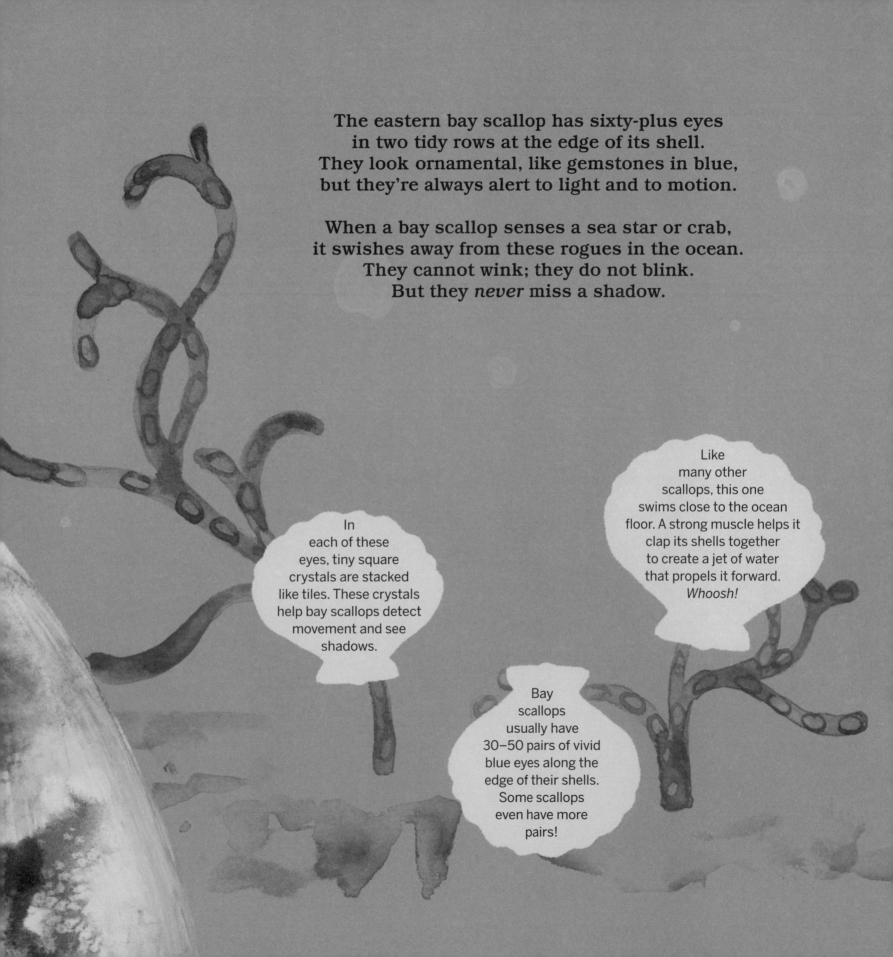

The eastern bay scallop has sixty-plus eyes
in two tidy rows at the edge of its shell.
They look ornamental, like gemstones in blue,
but they're always alert to light and to motion.

When a bay scallop senses a sea star or crab,
it swishes away from these rogues in the ocean.
They cannot wink; they do not blink.
But they *never* miss a shadow.

In each of these eyes, tiny square crystals are stacked like tiles. These crystals help bay scallops detect movement and see shadows.

Like many other scallops, this one swims close to the ocean floor. A strong muscle helps it clap its shells together to create a jet of water that propels it forward. *Whoosh!*

Bay scallops usually have 30–50 pairs of vivid blue eyes along the edge of their shells. Some scallops even have more pairs!

The common kingfisher is tiny and shy,
but it's a bird who plans swiftly when fish are nearby.
Perched on a twig, it knows to keep still
until just the right moment—
just one splintered second—
before some frisky wiggler is snatched in its bill.

Known for its
astonishing fishing
skills, this bird
can keep its head
still and its eyes
focused even when
other parts of its
body are bobbing in
the wind.

Once the
kingfisher spots its
prey, it uses sharp
visual measuring
skills to plunge
toward its
target.

It fixes its gaze on the river or stream
and waits with no flicker, no ruffle, no trill.
Then it drops through the air
with a flashing of blue and a flourish of gold.
Goodbye, little swimmer.
Good eye, keen fisher.

It's tricky work to
snap up a fish that's
always moving, but
this hunter can detect
fish through the
glare of sunlight and
the shifting hues of
moving water.

A dragonfly
has two immense eyes
with tens of thousands of lenses,
and each single lens sees a separate view of the world—
all on its own.

What a dragonfly sees must surely please,
since it detects far more colors than a human sees—
and not only that, but in almost three hundred and sixty degrees.
It's hard to catch a dragonfly:
it can still see you after it's flown by.

Dragonflies also have three
simple eyes on the tops of
their heads.

Except for one tiny spot right
behind them, dragonflies can see
in all directions at once.

Dragonflies have two gigantic
compound eyes that have as many
as 30,000 lenses—
and no eyelids.

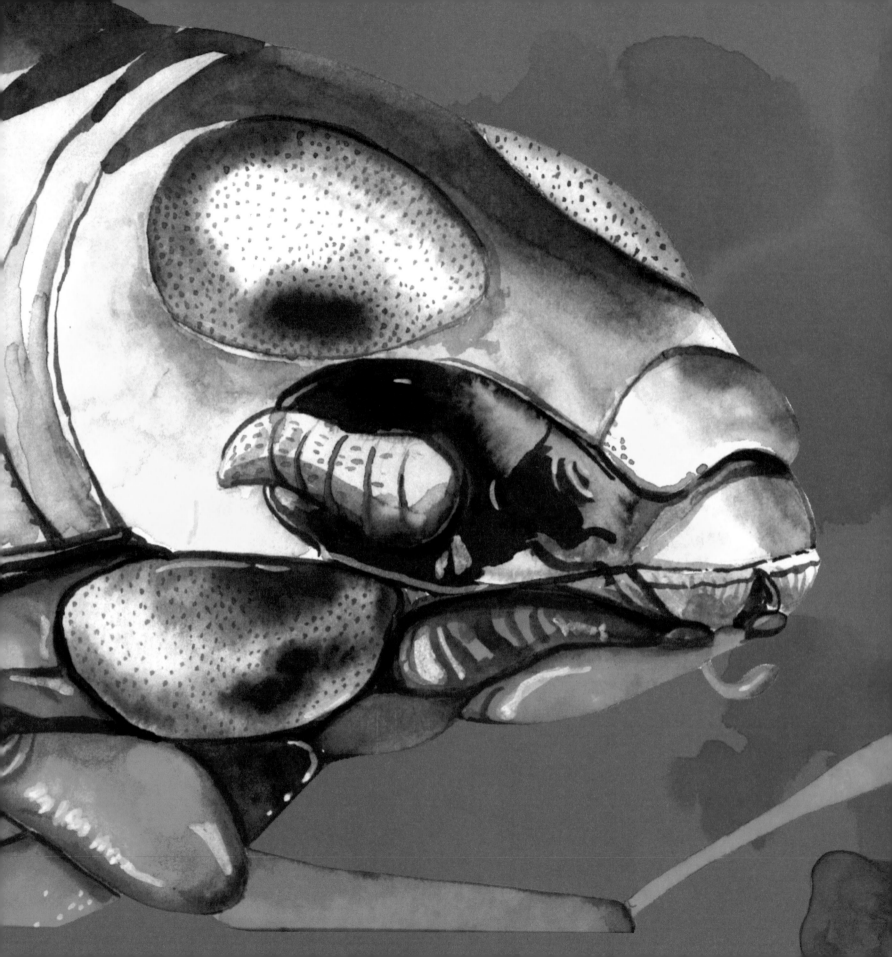

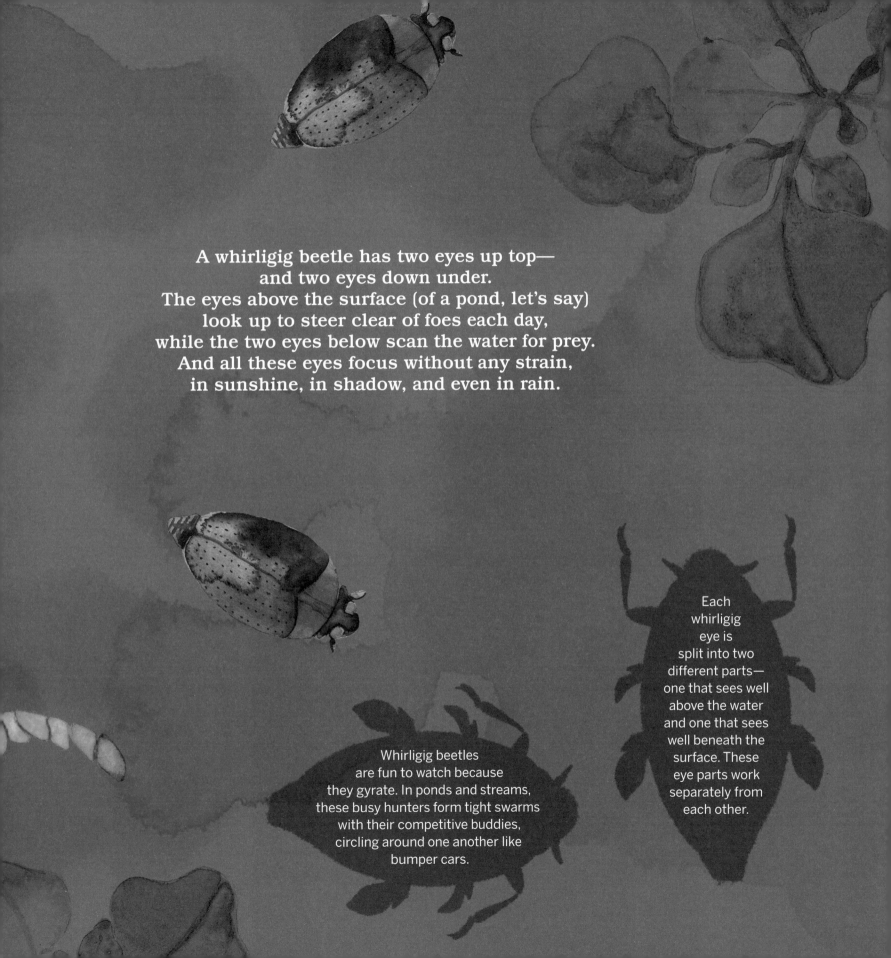

A whirligig beetle has two eyes up top—
and two eyes down under.
The eyes above the surface (of a pond, let's say)
look up to steer clear of foes each day,
while the two eyes below scan the water for prey.
And all these eyes focus without any strain,
in sunshine, in shadow, and even in rain.

Whirligig beetles
are fun to watch because
they gyrate. In ponds and streams,
these busy hunters form tight swarms
with their competitive buddies,
circling around one another like
bumper cars.

Each
whirligig
eye is
split into two
different parts—
one that sees well
above the water
and one that sees
well beneath the
surface. These
eye parts work
separately from
each other.

The eyes of an American bullfrog
beam brightly wherever they peer.
Bulging like headlights with three windshield washers,
they rise from its skull like knots on a log.

In the darkness of night, we may see them,
a-blink at the rim of a pond.
These eyes catch the glow of moonshine and stars
and toss it right back
toward the trouts' eyes—and ours.

Like all frogs, the
American bullfrog
has three eyelids
that clean and
protect its eyes.

At night an orangey-yellow
light called "eyeshine"
reflects from a layer of tissue
behind the frog's retina. This
glowing light helps the frog
to see its prey.

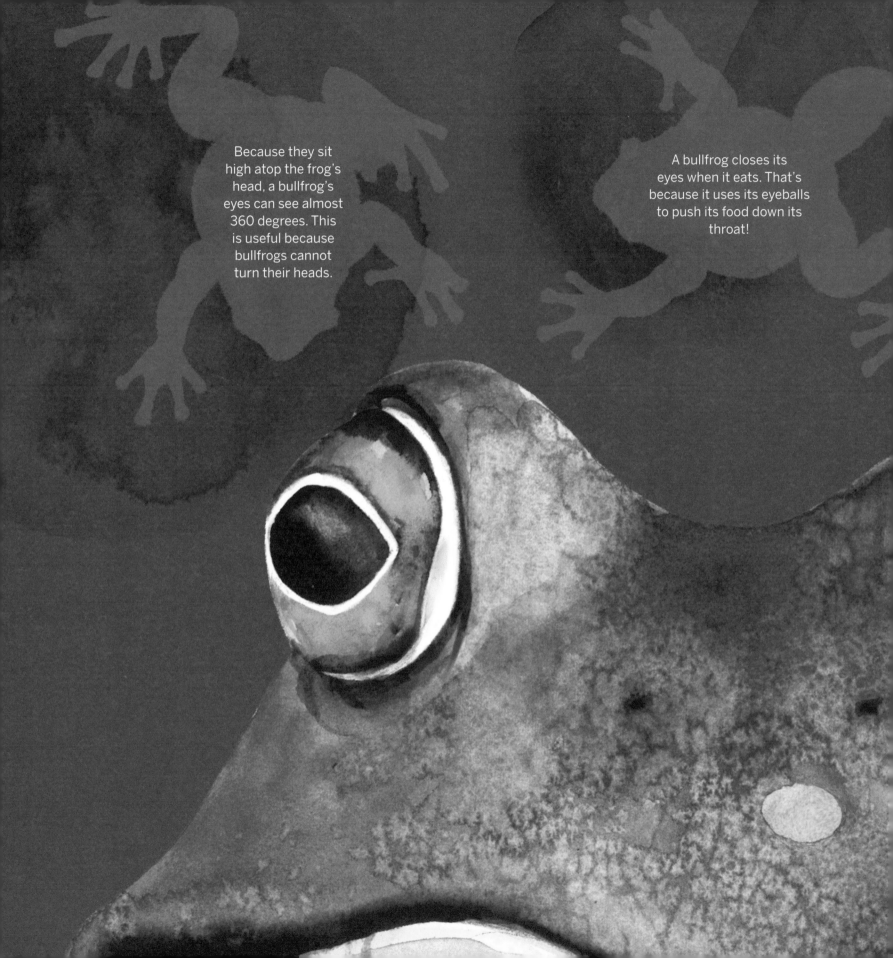

Because they sit high atop the frog's head, a bullfrog's eyes can see almost 360 degrees. This is useful because bullfrogs cannot turn their heads.

A bullfrog closes its eyes when it eats. That's because it uses its eyeballs to push its food down its throat!

A cheetah is no cat to mess with—
ask any gazelle on the African plains.
It will spot you and track you and chase you down,
for this is a cat who means business
from the cut-the-glare streaks of its tear lines
to the tip of its rudder-like tail.

This cat goes stalking at daybreak;
this cat goes prowling at dusk.
Its extra-sharp eyes keep a bead on its dinner—
and unless you are clever or maximally swift,
most of the time, the cheetah's the winner.

The cheetah's distinctive "tear lines," running from
the corners of each eye to the mouth, are black
hairs that may reduce the sun's glare and help the
cheetah hunt in bright light.

Only hawks and owls have sharper vision
than the cheetah, which can see detail as
far away as 2–3 miles in the dry forest or
treeless plains.

The cheetah is the world's fastest land animal. In
short sprints of up to 450 yards, it can reach speeds
up to 70 mph in three seconds.

The Union Island gecko cannot blink.
It has no eyelids (though some geckos do)
and no sliding membrane
to wipe away dust or other discomforts.

Instead it has two immovable brilles.
These clear-as-glass scales protect its eyes
as it hides beside boulders and searches the skies
for signs of the dangers that threaten its life.

When the brilles become grimy or stickily smudged,
this wizard lizard just sticks out its licker
and swipes at each eyeball until it is slicker.

Geckos may be 350 times more sensitive to light than
humans, so some geckos may be able to see color clearly at
night, especially under moonlight or starlight.

The Union Island gecko, which is about the
same size as a small paper clip, is one of
Earth's most endangered animals.

Jumping spiders—all six thousand species—excel at seeing and leaping.
With four pairs of eyes that work much like a spyglass,
they check out the scene in every direction.
Then they plan their moves with focused intention.

Their retinas swivel and sort information
until the front pair of eyes gets fixed on a target—
an ant or a fly or maybe a mate—
and then that spider gets ready to pounce
while its brain plans a leap that can't fail.

Each eye has an immovable lens attached to the outside of the spider's head. This lens collects light and sends it to each retina.

A jumping spider has eight eyes, arranged in pairs at the front, sides, and back of its head.

Each retina can move in all directions, so the spider can see in great detail without moving its head.

An owl on the prowl is no joker.
It's a serious, imperious hunter.
It's looking for mice and for skunks and for voles
at dawn or in evening, when twilight unrolls—
and shadows make timid beasts brave.

On velvety wings, owl comes gliding,
silent and stealthy and generally grim.
If you are a mouse or a rabbit,
you'll be the supper—not him.

Like other owls, the great horned owl cannot
move its eyes, but its head can turn up to 270
degrees, so it can look in any direction.

This owl usually hunts at dawn and dusk, but it has excellent
vision in daylight, dim light, and darkness.

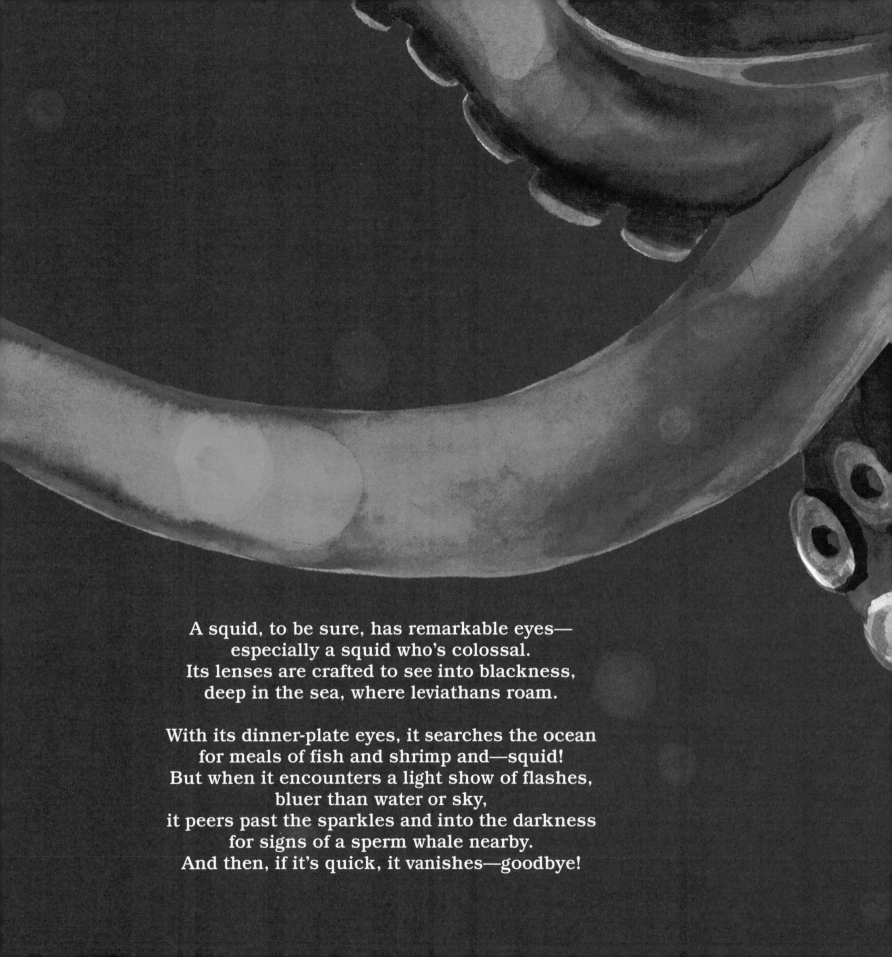

A squid, to be sure, has remarkable eyes—
especially a squid who's colossal.
Its lenses are crafted to see into blackness,
deep in the sea, where leviathans roam.

With its dinner-plate eyes, it searches the ocean
for meals of fish and shrimp and—squid!
But when it encounters a light show of flashes,
bluer than water or sky,
it peers past the sparkles and into the darkness
for signs of a sperm whale nearby.
And then, if it's quick, it vanishes—goodbye!

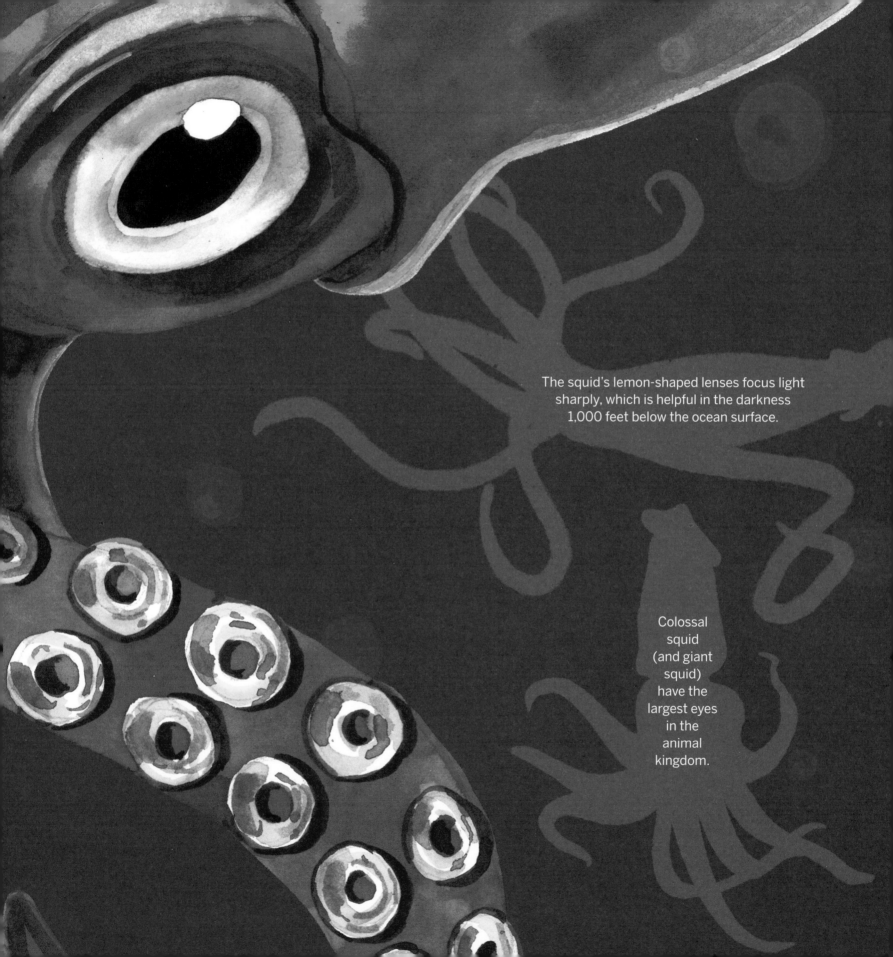

The squid's lemon-shaped lenses focus light sharply, which is helpful in the darkness 1,000 feet below the ocean surface.

Colossal squid (and giant squid) have the largest eyes in the animal kingdom.

When chameleons awaken, their eye cones start whirling.
One eye might ogle a worm on a leaf,
while the other's off gawking at crickets.
These eyeballs are famed for their fierce independence,
so they'll scout for a meal with two pupils swirling.

In tropical lowlands on the isle Madagascar,
scientists study the startling features
of these most outlandishly colorful creatures.
This lizard, for instance, can alter its hues
when it's threatened or cranky or cold.
And when snacks wander near, it shoots out its snatcher—
Earth's quickest and stickiest tongue.

Each of the
chameleon's eyes
can move on its
own—so this reptile
can focus on two
objects or places at
one time.

A chameleon focuses its eyes on its prey
and unleashes its superbly fast and sticky
tongue. Chameleon saliva is 400 times
thicker than human saliva.

But what about *you*?
What do *your* eyes do?

The eyeballs of humans are large, and they're round,
but the shapes of our eyelids may change how they look.
Sheltered in sockets, they move leftward
and rightward and upward and down.

They allow us to scan and to scout and survey
through the rosiest dawn and the glare of midday.
And though they are challenged when light disappears,
they keep trying to see whatever they can.

Our irises tend to be blue, green, or brown,
or maybe they're amber or hazel or gray.
A few of us have one eye that's brown and one that is blue.
And you? What hues have you?

We're born with eyelashes and eyebrows and lids—
and most of us blink ten thousand times in each day.
Blink.
Blink-blink
Blink-blink-blink.

You might see best when you look far away,
while a friend might see well when she looks close at hand.
But in all of us who are able to see,
there's a clear path
from every scene that enters our pupils
to the parts of our brains
where we sort through each image
to make sense of our world.

Most of the time,
while we sort, we think.
And we learn.
And we blink.
Blink.
Blink-blink.
Blink-blink-blink.

Or no blink.
Zzzzzzz...

How Your Eyes Work

All the different parts of your eyes work together to help you see.

The sclera is the tough white outer layer of the eyeball that gives it strength.

The cornea is the clear outer layer of the eye. It is shaped like a dome or like the crystal cover of a wristwatch.

The iris has muscles that adjust the size of the pupil to the amount of light. It is the colored part of the eye behind the cornea.

At the center of the iris is the pupil, an opening that controls the amount of light that enters the eye.

The lens is a clear inner part of the eye. It's flexible, and works with the cornea to focus light as the eye looks at objects.

The vitreous body, often called the vitreous humor, fills the space between the lens and the retina. It's filled with a clear, jelly-like material which gives the eye its shape.

Light passes through the vitreous humor to the retina, a light-sensitive layer of tissue. Special cells called photoreceptors turn the light into electrical signals.

The electrical signals travel through the optic nerve to the brain, which turns the signals into images that you see.

Tear glands above the eyeballs produce tears that your eyes need to work correctly. Every time you blink—about 10,000 times each day—the tears wash your eyes. The tears then flow into little canals that go to your nose. Sometimes, the tears can spill down your cheeks.

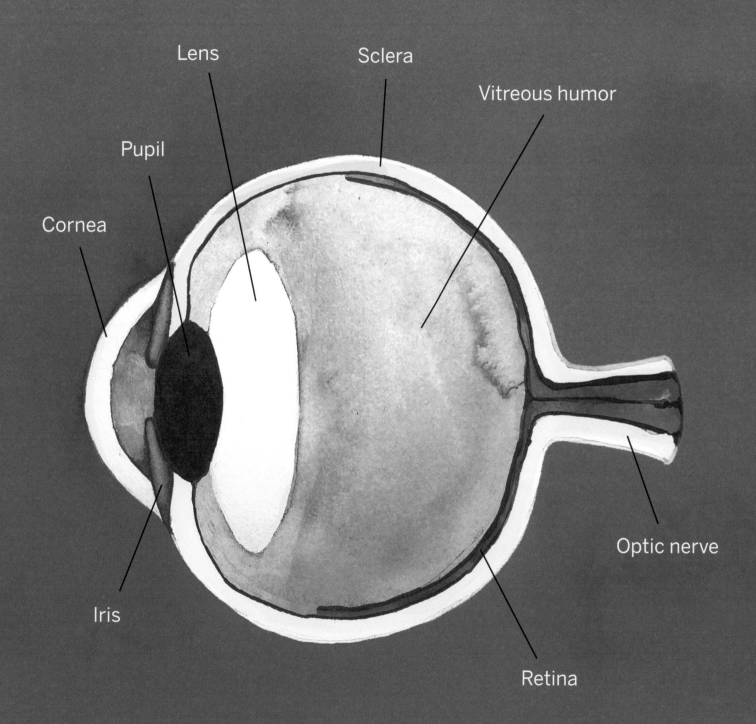

Lens

Sclera

Vitreous humor

Pupil

Cornea

Iris

Optic nerve

Retina

Author's Note

The idea for *Blink* came to me with a sudden new insight that the differing vision of certain animals, like the sharp-eyed hawks who pester my chickens, might be related to differences in the structures of their eyes. This moment led me toward studies of how animals see and what makes each animal's vision unique. In this exploration of the eyes and vision of some rare and familiar species, I learned that every kind of eye in the world has adapted to the habitat, the behaviors, and the needs of each seeing creature. The structures around and within each eye are designed in special ways that help preserve each animal's existence on Earth.

Resources

books for children

Duprat, Guillaume. *Eye Spy: Wild Ways Animals See the World.* Greenbelt, MD: What on Earth Publishing, 2018.

Jenkins, Steve. *Eye to Eye: How Animals See the World.* New York: Houghton Mifflin Harcourt, 2014.

Macaulay, David. *Eye: How It Works.* 2nd ed. New York: Roaring Brook, 2015.

Simon, Seymour. *Eyes and Ears.* New York: HarperCollins, 2005.

Young, Cybèle. *The Queen's Shadow: A Story about How Animals See.* Toronto: Kids Can, 2015.

books for adults

Ings, Simon. *A Natural History of Seeing: The Art and Science of Vision.* New York: W. W. Norton, 2007.

Land, Michael F., and Dan-Eric Nilsson. *Animal Eyes.* 2nd ed. New York: Oxford University Press, 2012.

Parker, Steve. *Color and Vision: The Evolution of Eyes and Perception.* Richmond Hill, ON: Firefly, 2016.

Glossary

brille: a clear, disc-shaped, immovable scale that covers each eye of most snakes and geckos.

choroid: the thin layer of blood vessels between the eyeball's retina and the sclera. It supplies blood and oxygen to the retina, and it absorbs light.

compound eye: an eye composed of hundreds or thousands of tiny tubelike structures that work together. These light-sensitive elements each form a portion of an image.

cones: light-sensitive cells that help the eye to see in bright light and to see color. Humans have about six million cones in each retina.

cornea: the clear dome that covers the front of the eyeball. It focuses light so images look sharp.

iris: the circular band of muscles that adjusts the size of the pupil to regulate the amount of light that enters the eye. It is the colored part of the eye.

lens: the clear tissue behind the iris that helps to focus light on the retina. It can bend to allow the eye to focus on objects both near and far away.

predator: a creature that hunts and eats other animals for food.

prey: an animal that is hunted and eaten by other animals.

pupil: the opening at the center of the iris.

retina: the layer of tissue at the back of the eyeball that contains cells that are responsive to light. It converts the images received by the lens into electrical signals that are sent to the brain.

rods: light-sensitive cells that help the eye to see in low light. Humans have about 120 million rods in each retina.

sclera: the protective white outer coating of the eye. It is also known as "the white of the eye."

simple eye: an eye having a single lens.

tissue: the material, made up of similar cells, that forms the parts of a plant or the parts of the body in an animal.

vitreous humor: the clear gel that fills the inside of the eyeball and helps it keep its shape.

For Caleb Gonzalez—ophthalmologist and kindest of human beings—
with deepest gratitude for his tender care of someone I dearly love—DB

To my husband, who is always patient with me during our walks
when I suddenly stop to draw a flower...for two hours—AL

Library of Congress Cataloging-in-Publication data is on file with the publisher.

Text copyright © 2020 Doe Boyle

Illustrations copyright © 2020 by Albert Whitman & Company

Illustrations by Adèle Leyris

First published in the United States of America in 2020 by Albert Whitman & Company

ISBN 978-0-8075-0667-7 (hardcover)

ISBN 978-0-8075-0674-5 (ebook)

Printed in China

10 9 8 7 6 5 4 3 2 1 WKT 24 23 22 21 20

Design by Rick DeMonico

For more information about Albert Whitman & Company,
visit our website at www.albertwhitman.com